Forensic Crime Solvers

CAUSE OF DEATH

By Barbara B. Rollins and Michael Dahl

Consultant:
Eric A. Evans, M.D.
Anatomical and Clinical Pathologist
Immanuel St Joseph's-Mayo Health System
Mankato, Minnesota

Capstone *press*
Mankato, Minnesota

Edge Books are published by Capstone Press
151 Good Counsel Drive, P.O. Box 669, Mankato, Minnesota 56002
www.capstonepress.com

Library of Congress Cataloging-in-Publication Data
Rollins, Barbara B.
     Cause of death / by Barbara B. Rollins and Michael Dahl.
     p. cm.—(Edge books. Forensic crime solvers)
     Summary: Describes clues bodies leave behind about the cause of death, procedures
for autopsies, and ways medical examiners form an opinion about how a death
has occurred.
     Includes bibliographical references and index.
     ISBN 0-7368-2420-0 (hardcover)
     1. Medical jurisprudence—Juvenile literature. 2. Forensic sciences—Juvenile
literature. [1. Medical jurisprudence. 2. Forensic sciences.] I. Dahl, Michael. II. Title.
III. Series.
RA1063.R635 2004
614' .1—dc22   2003013030

Editorial Credits
Carrie Braulick, editor; Juliette Peters, designer; Jo Miller, photo researcher

Photo Credits
Capstone Press/Gary Sundermeyer, 4, 7, 8
Corbis, 16; Australian Picture Library, cover; Reuters NewMedia Inc./Paul
     McErlane, 12; SABA/Shepard Sherbell, 13, 18, 26, 28; Sygma, 23
Getty Images Inc./Mario Villafuerte, 24
Stockbyte, 15
Photo Researchers Inc./Costantino Margiotta, 22; Science Photo Library/Pascal
     Goetgheluck, 10, 14
PhotoDisc Inc., 21
Unicorn Stock Photos/Jeff Greenberg, 1; M. Siluk, 20

**Capstone Press thanks David B. Petersen, assistant laboratory director
at the Minnesota Bureau of Criminal Apprehension, for his help in
preparing this book.**

1 2 3 4 5 6 09 08 07 06 05 04

Table of Contents

CHAPTER 1

Learn about:

- Crime scene investigators
- Medical examiners
- Ligature marks

The Body
in the Forest

On a windy August afternoon, two hikers were exploring the woods in a state park. They followed a narrow trail. One of the hikers saw a squirrel run into the bushes. Then the other hiker noticed something small and pale at the side of the trail. It looked like a hand. The hikers took a few more steps. They saw a man's body behind thick brush. The hikers checked to see if the man was injured. He was not breathing and had no pulse. The man was dead.

The Investigation Team

The hikers ran to the park's information office. They told the workers what they had seen. Park workers called the local police station. Soon, police officers, crime scene investigators (CSIs), a medical examiner (ME), and a homicide detective arrived. The two hikers led the group to the body. The detective and investigators searched for clues.

◄ Hikers can be the first people to find a crime scene.

A First Look

The ME stepped toward the body to begin her investigation. She photographed the body and pulled on a pair of latex gloves.

The ME looked for clues that showed when and how the man died. She noticed that the man's body was stiff. Because of the body stiffness, she decided the man had been dead for more than three hours. Straight purple lines circled the back of the man's neck. She also noticed a small bruise on his neck. The ME examined these ligature marks. She thought that the man had been strangled with a piece of rope or wire. She thought the small bruise may have been formed by a knot or loop in the rope or wire.

After her quick examination, the ME taped paper bags around the man's hands. The bags would prevent damage to any evidence on the hands. An investigator helped the ME place the body into a large plastic bag. They put the body in the ME's van. The ME drove the van to the morgue.

MEs may work with
homicide detectives
at crime scenes.

MEs complete an autopsy report after they determine a cause of death.

The Autopsy

At the morgue, the ME performed an autopsy. She took samples of the man's blood. She checked the skin for bruises and other marks. She noticed small scratches on the man's hands and arms. The ME pulled nylon fibers out of the man's neck bruise. She also examined the man's heart, lungs, and other organs.

After the autopsy, the ME considered the evidence she had found. She decided the death was probably a homicide. She believed the man died after an attacker tightened a nylon rope or cord around his neck. The rope cut off the man's oxygen supply, causing his death.

The ME finished her autopsy report. She explained her report to the homicide detective in charge of the case. The detective now had another case to solve.

CHAPTER 2

Learn about:

- Types of wounds
- Rigor mortis
- Gunshot residue

Manner of Death

MEs are doctors trained to find a person's cause and manner of death. Cause of death is the medical reason why a person died. For example, an ME might decide that a person died from lack of oxygen or heart disease.

Manner of death is a legal reason explaining a person's death. MEs can report at least four manners of death. These manners are homicide, suicide, accidental, and natural. In some states and counties, MEs also can report an unknown, or undetermined, manner of death.

MEs perform careful investigations before they make a decision about manner of death. They consider clues from crime scenes. The location and position of a body when it was found are important clues.

Investigators take photos of evidence
◀ after a body is found.

Investigators at crime scenes where a death occurred wear clothing that protects themselves and the evidence.

Homicide

Homicide, or murder, is the willful killing of one person by another. Homicide victims may be strangled, beaten, drowned, or poisoned. They also can be shot or stabbed.

Wounds can provide clues that a death was homicide. Knife wounds at the top of the back can suggest a homicide. People cannot easily stab themselves in this area. Bruises around the neck, or ligature marks, can indicate that a person was strangled. Indentations can show where a heavy object struck a victim.

Scratches, cuts, and scrapes on a body's hands may be defensive wounds. These wounds happen when a victim fights against an attacker.

After an ME determines a death was homicide, a homicide detective searches for suspects. The detective may use information from the ME's autopsy report to help in the investigation.

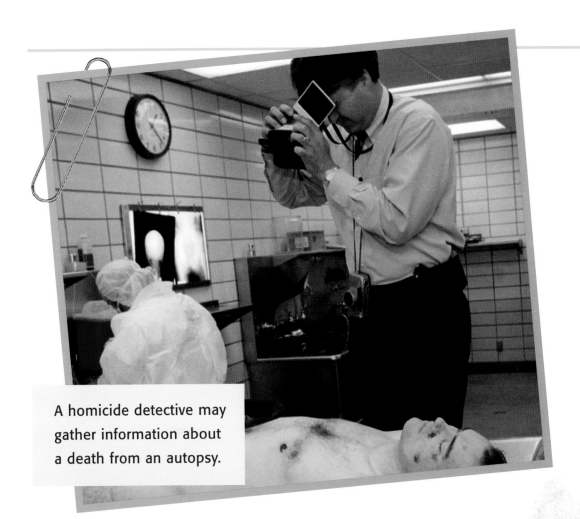

A homicide detective may gather information about a death from an autopsy.

Time of Death

Part of an ME's job is to estimate a person's time of death. The time of death can help investigators find out more about what happened at a crime scene.

MEs consider the development of rigor mortis when determining time of death. About three hours after death, a body stiffens. The stiffening first affects small muscles, such as muscles in the face, jaw, and neck. The hardness then spreads to the rest of the body. After about 12 hours, rigor mortis is usually in its final stages.

After rigor mortis, the muscle tissues begin to break down. They soften and relax in the same order that they first became stiff. About 30 hours after death, a body is completely relaxed.

Insects also can help an ME determine time of death. A dead body attracts blowflies, beetles, and other insects. An ME can examine the type of insects and their stages of development to help estimate time of death.

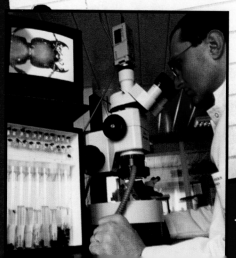

The study of insects can help
◄ MEs determine time of death.

Suicide

Suicides occur when people kill themselves on purpose. It is a leading manner of death in the United States. The number of suicides is especially high for people ages 15 to 24.

Even if a death appears to be a suicide, CSIs and MEs keep investigating. A killer may try to make a homicide look like a suicide. CSIs may check for gunshot residue on the body. This mixture of partly-burned particles sprays out of a gun when it fires. CSIs and MEs also can consider the angle of the wounds or the body's position to determine if a death was suicide.

Accidental and Natural Deaths

Unexpected deaths are accidental. Accidents include car crashes, plane crashes, and falls at work sites. Farm workers have a high rate of accidental deaths. They work around dangerous equipment.

Several clues can suggest an accidental death. A choking victim might have food stuck in the throat. A person who died from a fall often has head injuries.

Natural death occurs as a result of a sickness or a normal process. Autopsy results may show that the person who died had a fatal disease. MEs also may notice organ damage inside a body.

Injuries that occur from automobile accidents are one of the main causes
◀ of death in the United States.

CHAPTER 3

Learn about:

- Autopsy procedures
- Examining the organs
- Lab tests

The Autopsy

MEs perform autopsies at hospitals or medical centers. Autopsies help them determine how a person died. Autopsies are often performed after mysterious deaths. State laws require an autopsy if officials believe the manner of death was homicide.

During an autopsy, MEs follow certain steps. They photograph the outside of the body. They take x-rays to produce photos of the inside of the body. X-rays can reveal broken bones or objects inside the body. MEs then perform external and internal examinations.

External Clues

MEs closely examine the outside of a body during an autopsy. They look for wounds and bruises on the skin. They also examine the head. A bloody bruise, cut, or indentation on the head can sometimes explain how a person died.

◀ MEs weigh organs during autopsies.

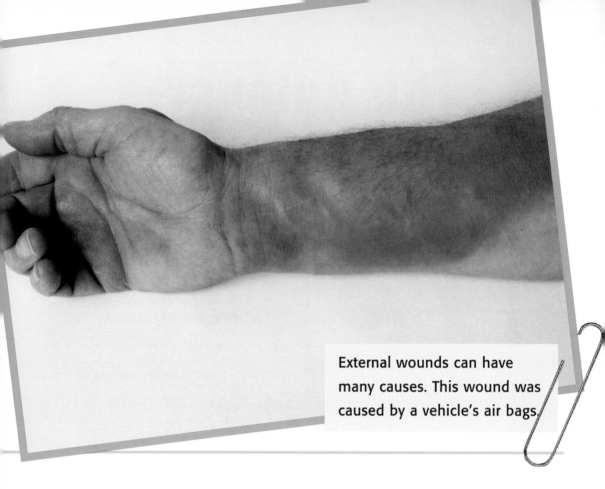

External wounds can have many causes. This wound was caused by a vehicle's air bags.

The eyes also can provide clues about death. The dark center of the eye, called the pupil, becomes larger when a person is struck on the side of the head. Enlarged pupils also can show the presence of drugs in the victim's body. They may be a clue that the person died of a drug overdose.

MEs may be able to determine the type of weapon involved in a death. Deep cuts and slashes indicate a knife attack. Small round indentations on the skin can suggest that an attacker used a hammer.

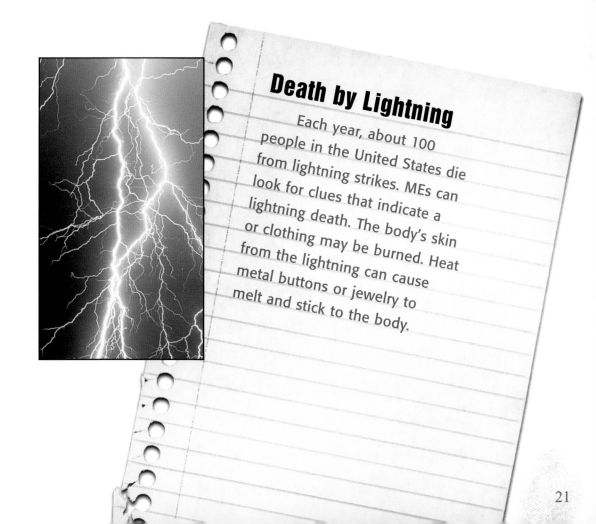

Death by Lightning

Each year, about 100 people in the United States die from lightning strikes. MEs can look for clues that indicate a lightning death. The body's skin or clothing may be burned. Heat from the lightning can cause metal buttons or jewelry to melt and stick to the body.

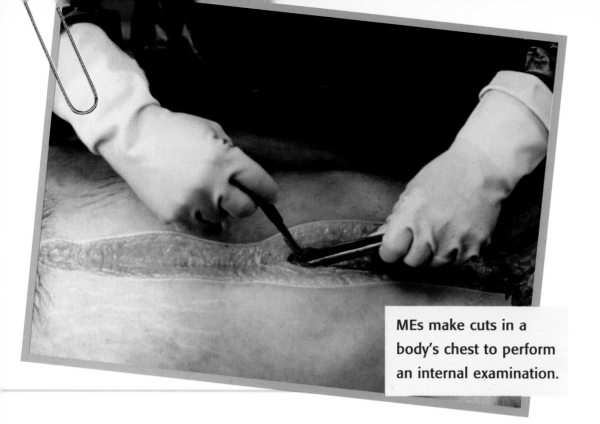

MEs make cuts in a body's chest to perform an internal examination.

Internal Examination

After the external examination, MEs examine the body's internal parts. MEs make three deep cuts in the body's chest and abdomen. These cuts form the shape of a *Y*. The skin is pulled back and held in place with clamps. MEs then look for injuries inside the body. A victim of a knife attack may have cuts in the organs. A poison called cyanide causes the stomach lining to break down.

MEs examine the lungs, stomach, liver, and other organs. They check to see if the organs have a normal color. A victim of heart disease may have tan coloring on the heart. MEs also check the weight of the organs. Drowning victims or victims of heart failure may have extra fluid in the lungs. Extra fluid causes the lungs to weigh more than healthy lungs.

People who die from head wounds often have suffered brain injuries. MEs use a small saw to cut into the skull during an autopsy. They look for tears, swelling, and bleeding in the brain.

MEs closely examine the head for signs of injury.

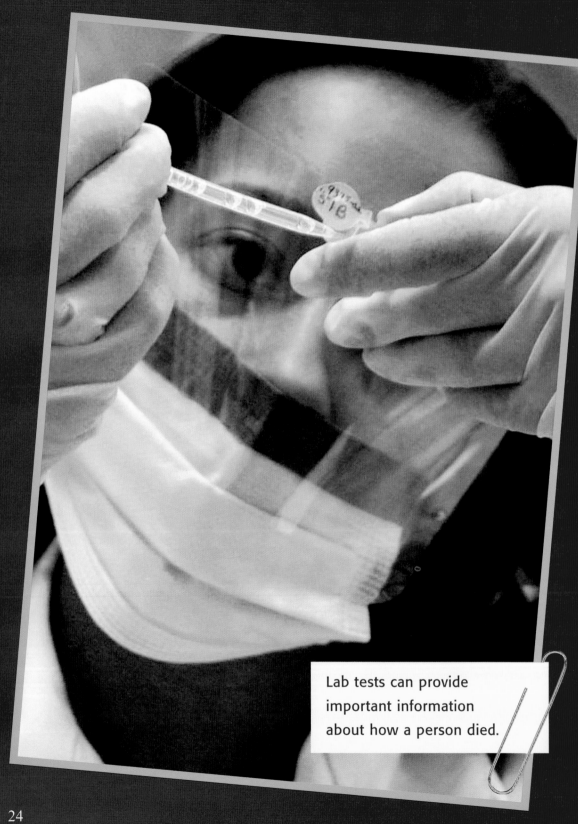

Lab tests can provide important information about how a person died.

Lab Testing

MEs take samples of blood and organ tissue during an autopsy. These samples are sent to a lab for testing.

Lab results can help MEs determine cause or manner of death. A blood sample may show drugs in the blood. An organ tissue sample can show signs of a disease.

Second Autopsies

Sometimes detectives working on old cases find out new information about a death. They may believe an autopsy was not complete. They may want to dig up a buried body for a second autopsy.

A second autopsy may not reveal as much information as the first. A dead body's tissue breaks down quickly. But second autopsies still can provide clues about how a person died.

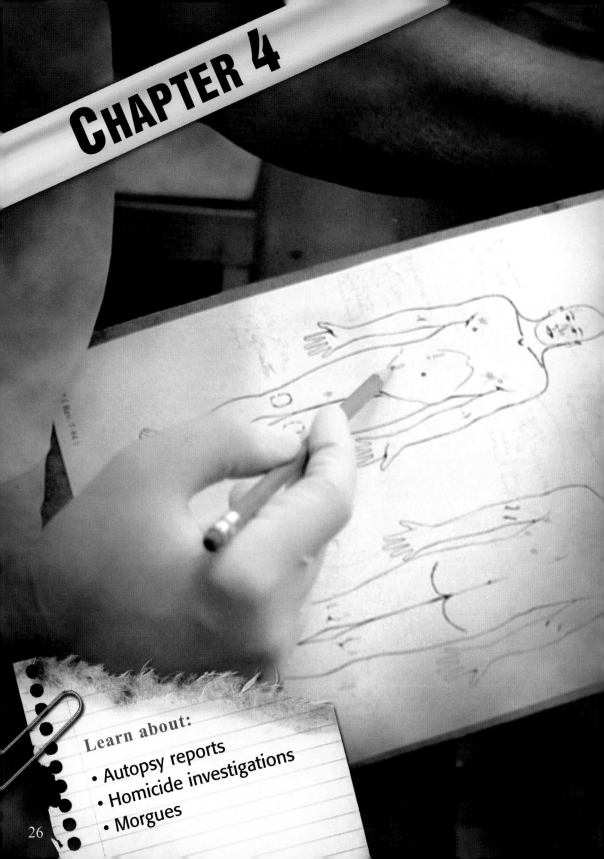

CHAPTER 4

Learn about:

- Autopsy reports
- Homicide investigations
- Morgues

After the Autopsy

An autopsy can last from one hour to a day or more. An ME may need less time to examine a victim with one wound than a victim with many wounds. After a body has been examined, MEs prepare a report about how the person died.

Using Autopsy Results

An autopsy report must be as accurate and complete as possible. It usually includes both gross and microscopic results. Gross results include information from an ME's external examination. Microscopic results include information about blood and other samples taken from the body.

MEs sometimes speak about autopsy results for homicide investigations in court. They report the facts about autopsies and answer questions based on their results.

◄ MEs carefully record their findings after autopsies.

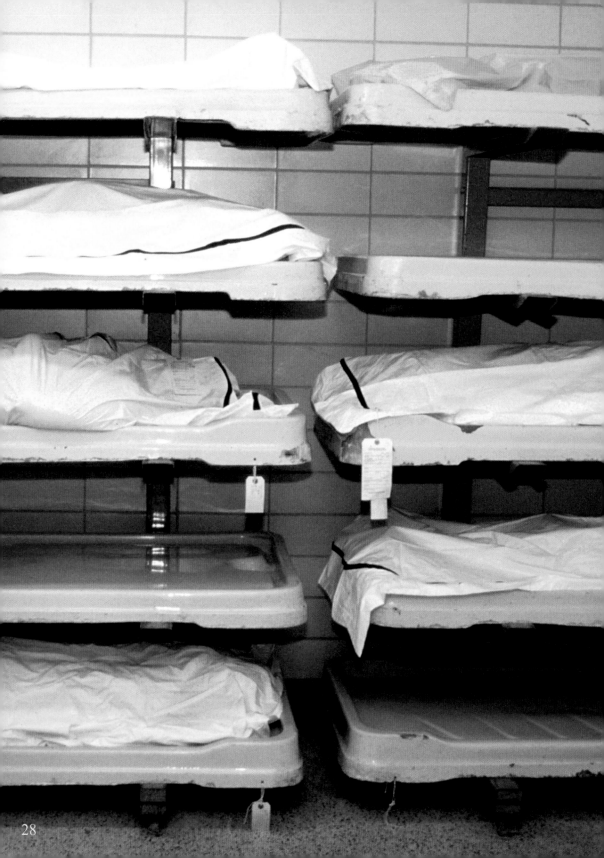

Storing Bodies

Bodies are usually kept at morgues before and after autopsies. Morgues usually have refrigerated lockers built into the walls. Each locker has a sliding tray or table that holds a body. Air in the lockers is about 35 to 46 degrees Fahrenheit (2 to 8 degrees Celsius). The cool temperature helps keep the bodies from breaking down.

Bodies can be kept in morgue lockers for about four days. After this time, they usually are taken to a mortuary. Workers at the mortuary prepare the body for a funeral.

Each death is important to an ME. They know that law enforcement officials, the families of deceased people, and many others rely on the results of their work.

◀ Dead bodies are stored at morgues.

Glossary

autopsy (AW-top-see)—an examination performed on a dead body to find the cause and manner of death

evidence (EV-uh-duhnss)—information, items, and facts that help prove something is true or false

homicide (HOM-uh-side)—the willful killing of one person by another person

ligature mark (LIG-uh-chur MARK)—a mark indicating that something was tied tightly around the neck

medical examiner (MED-uh-kuhl eg-ZAM-uh-nur)—a public officer trained to study bodies to determine a cause and manner of death

morgue (MORG)—a place where dead bodies are kept until they are identified or released for burial

rigor mortis (RI-gor MOR-tuhs)—temporary stiffness of muscles occurring after death

Read More

Friedlander, Mark P. Jr., and Terry M. Phillips. *When Objects Talk: Solving a Crime with Science.* Minneapolis: Lerner, 2001.

Murdico, Suzanne J. *Forensic Scientists: Life Investigating Sudden Death.* Extreme Careers. New York: Rosen, 2003.

Platt, Richard. *Crime Scene: The Ultimate Guide to Forensic Science.* New York: DK Publishing, 2003.

Yeatts, Tabatha. *Forensics: Solving the Crime.* Innovators. Minneapolis: Oliver Press, 2001.

Useful Addresses

National Association of Medical Examiners
430 Pryor Street SW
Atlanta, GA 30312

National Center for Forensic Science
University of Central Florida
P.O. Box 162367
Orlando, FL 32816-2367

Internet Sites

FactHound offers a safe, fun way to find Internet sites related to this book. All of the sites on FactHound have been researched by our staff.

Here's how:

1. Visit www.facthound.com
2. Type in this special code **0736824200** for age-appropriate sites. Or enter a search word related to this book for a more general search.
3. Click on the **Fetch It** button.

FactHound will fetch the best sites for you!

Index